he loves me,
he loves me not enough

cammie dennis

for the love of all man kind

dear reader,

I hope this book finds you with more love in your heart than I once had for myself – *it is a gift to feel love.*

Ever since I was a little girl, I've always known myself to be a very deeply feeling human being. Throughout my most formative years, I quickly learned that not everyone experiences the world the same way that I do – not everyone feels as deeply as I do. Although this is something that I have grown to love, I spent most of my adolescent life trying to hide it.

Somewhere along the way, I learned to numb myself to the feeling of love – and any other feeling for that matter. I thought that it would protect me from the world around me – the world that tried to tell me how I should be. I let society convince me that to feel everything is a "bad" thing, and that to be sensitive is to be "weak". It took me years to realize that this is far from the truth. The truth is that to feel your emotions with every part of you, to allow others to see you for who you truly are, and to have a heart that leads with love – that is a gift, and I intend not to waste it. It is who I am, and who I have always been, and I have learned to not only embrace it, but to unconditionally love it.

Three years ago, I set out on a journey to heal my own heart, and throughout that time, I found myself enamored by beautiful poetry. The words that I read made me feel things that I had not felt in years – they brought me back to the best parts of me. They taught me that to feel my emotions with such intensity is not a weakness, but rather, my greatest strength. They reminded me that to be real is to be beautiful – and to love is to live. These words brought me back into my own, and they healed the parts of me that I thought I had lost in my adolescence.

And now I am here in hopes that I can do the same for you.

Throughout my life, I have experienced many different types of love, but one stood out more than the rest. This love taught me more about myself than anything else. I learned that love is not just one thing – it is everything, and it is all around us. I learned that love exists in every person you meet, because love exists within you. But most importantly, I learned that if you have to choose between loving yourself or loving another – always choose you.

The poetry in this book tells my side of the love story – from falling in love, to falling apart and ultimately coming back to the love of my own heart. The words that I write are made for people like me – the ones who can't help but to wear their hearts on their sleeves.

–

And so I'll leave you with this:

Be kind to others, but always be kind to yourself. Remember, love is important and love heals. Love recklessly and wildly– and always stay true to who you are. Your love is important – and so are you.

from my heart to yours, with love

cammie

love me through the night

he loves me, he loves me not enough

that's what our summer was all about

– *open windows*
and midnight kisses

lay me gently to rest tonight
I am all yours
    – and you are all mine

in a matter of minutes
he touched parts of me that no one ever had
he reached out with both hands
and gripped onto the deepest parts of my soul
– *I remember it like it was yesterday,*
there was something about him that made me feel whole

my body is my own
but for tonight
I will lend her to you

please show her love
– she has not always been cherished
for what she was,
but only ever desired
for what she does

you must be warned
before you touch me
I have scars all over my body,
and I know they are not from you
but what I want to say
is to please be careful
with what you do

– only few have seen what she's been through

waking up next to you
felt nothing like it usually does
after a night out
there was no awkward goodbye
or small talk about the week ahead
no, not at all
waking up next to you
didn't feel like I was at someone else's house
– it felt like I was already home

I move for you

– every part of my body dances
at the thought of your lips on mine

look at you
with your half sleepy eyes
and 'kiss me one more time' smile

– you make sharp edges look smooth

here I am
with your body all over mine
and there's nothing around us
but the morning light,
as I lay here next to you
I can feel your heartbeat
all over me
and there's nothing between us
but thin white bed sheets,
I take one look in your eyes
and my head starts to spin
– I can't seem to figure out
where you end
and I begin

paint my body gold
and allow me to sing you my song

paint my body blue
and let me swim inside the depths of you

paint my body black
and promise me there's no going back

– I'm falling in love with all that we have

it wasn't love at first sight
but it was something close to it
it was as if the heart in me
recognized the heart in you
and I knew it was only a matter of time
until it was just me,
you,
and the moon

we spent the whole night on my kitchen floor,
drinking wine straight from the bottle
because we could
we made love in the bathroom
instead of the bed
because there was something about it
that felt better than the rest
we kissed
and we danced
and we fell in love
because days like this
are when we felt most like us.

we were so alive it almost hurt
– we were so alive
that flowers started to grow out of my heart

would you come here
and tell me you love me?

– boy, I am consumed by your body

dress me up in your best compliment
and then kiss me for all of our friends to see

– loving you is my favorite part of me

there was such an unusual thing about him
– he was the most destructive human being
that I had ever met
always finding a way to get himself
into some sort of mess
he had beautiful eyes
and calloused hands
and something about him
reminded me of who I am
he held my heart near and dear
always turning a blind eye
to what he feared
but nothing ever stopped him
from going after what he wanted
so he took me in
and asked me to listen
always protecting me
but only at an arm's distance
and still,
there was something so simple
about the way he laughed
and let me in
– it was such an unusual thing about him,

he destroyed everything that he could see
...except for me

you make me feel everything

*– I can't tell if I want to thank you for it
or if I want to kill you because of it*

there was something so intriguing
about his wide-eyed stare
and his beautiful grin

he had me undone in places
that were invisible
to everyone,

everyone
but him

you are love,

in my eyes
you are everything about love
that ever made sense to me
you are love
and coffee on a Sunday morning
and hot showers on a cold day
and all of the flowers that bloom in May

you are the only thing about love
that ever made sense to me
– you are the only thing about love
that ever made me
feel like me

rent free

my mother always told me
that when you find the one person in this world
whose weirdness matches your own,
keep them close

– how do I politely tell you
that you are the most
strangely, unique
human being
that I have ever met,
and it is every reason why
you are the only thing living
inside of my head?

loving you was quiet,
creeping up on me in the night

– in the midst of the moonlight
my heart chose you
and my mind lost the fight

to love you
is to say that I am prepared
to open myself up to you,
I've never opened up myself to anyone

please be gentle with what you see
– what I'm about to show you
is the rawest part of me

they say that you sleep easy
when you're with the one you love

*– my body must've known how I felt
before my mind could catch up*

for once in my life
I could finally shut my mind off
and just be
– your presence alone
allowed me to not have to think
and that is something so new to me

for once in my life
I actually felt free

and now I must confess
that my love for you
has grown
beyond anything I could ever imagine,
now I must confess
that I have always loved you
even before I knew what love could be

– even before there was a possibility
of 'you and me'

I dreamt of kissing you last night,
I awoke to the taste of your lips on mine

...and so I will spend
the rest of my days
tasting my wildest dreams

something more

our bodies are close
but our hearts are more
and so here we lay
with nothing between us

– nothing,
but the taste of something more

'oh no,
this must be love,"
my mind cried.

"*ah yes,*
I am finally home,"
my heart whispered back.

in my favorite diary
that reads, 'notebook' on the front cover
I took a permanent marker
and wrote,
"I think I love him"
"I think I'm falling in love with him"
– *everything about him is love*
and I am consumed by all of it

I'm so full on your love
– I haven't eaten since last Wednesday

I would love nothing more
than to be simply
and entirely
saturated by your existence

delicate words pour out of me
when I look into your eyes
there is a depth to them
that is beyond anything
I could ever find
the secrets that they keep
whisper sweet nothings
and I fall into the space
between everything
and nothing

– but with every look
and every heartbeat
I fall more in love
with who you are to me
and with every word
that your eyes speak
secrets spill out
like the way you pour your coffee

cammie dennis

no one has ever been able
to open me up
quite the way that you do

     – now I know that my whole summer
      will be spent loving you

there was nothing quite like
Cinnamon Toast Crunch
in the morning
and you
Cinnamon Toast Crunch
hot coffee
and you
Cinnamon Toast Crunch
hot coffee
cigarettes
and you
– there was nothing quite like you

and I woke up every morning
to nothing
but the taste
of you

drown me in all of your love

– you are the only thing I've ever prayed for

more of you,
that's all I need

I'm addicted to the feeling

of you loving you me

tequila soda with extra limes

I know my love is something
you have never seen
– *and yes,*
I would be scared of me
but when the bartender asked for my drink
you smiled and said,
'two tequila sodas
with extra limes"
– *and you looked at me*
like I was nothing to hide

and god
I'm so afraid
that you might not love me,

but it feels so good
for someone to want me

I would like to kiss you
in every beautiful place
that our souls can find

...you will taste my love
wherever you would like

his eyes speak words
that only my soul can comprehend

– every time I look inside
I fall in love
over
and over
and over again

I am bound to the essence
of who you are to me

— I am bound by your love
and there is no letting it be

you paint my roses red
when I thought I'd have to spend a lifetime
just being blue

– I didn't know someone could make me feel the way that you do

loving you is easy

I spent my my whole life thinking that love
was something you had to earn,
something you had to fight to get
and suffer to keep
something that made you give up pieces of yourself
for another human being

but then you showed up
and you reminded me that love is easy
– *loving you is easy*

you showed me that it can walk into your life
on a Tuesday afternoon
and say,
'you –
I pick you"
not because of who you are
or what you do
but because I want to love every version of you

you showed up
like no one ever had
and showed me that love isn't so bad

– *it's kind of sweet, actually*

my mind is a memory bank full of trauma
and you robbed me clean of everything I ever knew

– you healed the parts of me
that were once a shade of blue

if I write one poem everyday for a year
then I will have 365 ways to tell you how much I love you
if I write two poems everyday for a year
then i will have 730 ways to tell you how much I love you
if I write three poems everyday for a year
then I will have 1095 ways to tell you how much love you
and   so   on
and   so   forth

what I'm trying to say is that
ever since the day I met you
I haven't been able to write about anything
except for how much I love you
and I'd spend everyday
of the rest of our lives
writing millions of poems
to tell you how much I love you
cause god, do I love you
but even I know that words couldn't do the love justice

p.s. I fucking love you

     if love is a choice
     I choose you

     in this life
     and the next
     I think I may always
     choose you

     – and in this life,
     it has always been you

     .

     p.s. I fucking love you

I slip through the cracks of you
with every glance
and every kiss
reminds me that I am too soft
and too sensitive
to make it through a world like this
without you by my side

there you go again
picking up the pieces of me
I thought I had forgotten

– here I go again,
trying not to be the one
who ends up being forgotten

you are every part of me

I don't know if that makes sense to you,
but it makes sense to me

because every part of you
is the home I never knew I would need,
because the only words I can write
are about what your love does for me,
because all of you
has become
every part of me,
and from what I can see
even the most perfectly curated
strings of words
could never depict
that you are the only thing
I could ever need,
because you are
the only part of me
that I was ever missing

– and I don't know if that makes sense to you,
but you make sense to me

you are my moon

– I love you in all of your phases

2:00 am thoughts

you
– *you're the only thing that I think about*

oh how lovely it is
to kiss
and be in love

– oh how lovely it is
to kiss you
and be in love with you

he loves me, he loves me not enough

loving you never crossed my mind

...it lived there

the hopeless romantic

I hope our love never grows old
I hope that fifty years down the road
you are still the face I see
when I wake for the day
on a cold Monday morning
I hope you are the last person I see
after one too many drinks
and I hope your laugh
is the soundtrack to all of my stories
I hope your body is always beside me
and I hope my life is spent loving
the only one that could ever find me
– I hope that every day of the rest our lives
are spent loving each other
cause not a single thing in this world
could ever convince me to love another,
and I hope that the love
growing between us two
is nurtured by all of the days
I will spend loving you

to know you
is to love you
– but to know you like I do,
that is a goddamn miracle

you ask me what my favorite flower is
and expect me to have an answer
when the truth is
that is like asking me what I love most about you
– *there is no way to pick just one*
when something so beautiful
exists in so many different ways

"why me?"
he asked.

"because they're not you,"
I whispered back.

– *it's as simple*
and as complicated
as that

I never wanted to change you
I only ever wanted to love you
for exactly who you are

— because the best
and worst
parts of you
live in every part of my heart

if I tell you that I love you
would you hold it against me
like my loved ones did to me so many?

and maybe times have changed,
maybe you are not the same
– but if I tell you that I love you
would you call me insane?

in love, I am ours

my love looks like bringing you something
on a Tuesday
because I saw it at the grocery store
and thought of you
my love looks like kisses at all times of the day
because I can't get enough of you
my love looks like cuddles in bed
and flowers on the counter
it comes in all different colors
because in love,

I am ours

there isn't a damn thing you could do
that could make me fall out of love with you

– it seems to be
the only problem for me

loving you felt illegal

like going to the grocery store at 8 pm
or kissing your best friend when you're drunk

– *something about it felt like more than enough*

I'd let you break my heart a million times over

I wouldn't want you to,
but I'd let you

– and I think that says all I need it to

drinks on me

the drinks get stronger
and the lines get blurred
and somewhere between it all
I end up in your bed once more
and when the morning light shines through
I must remind myself
that it's just another morning
waking up next to you,
and days like this
never last quite as long
but tomorrow morning
it'll all be gone

...will you be gone, too?

drinks on me

you say you love wine
but you keep your favorite bottle
on the shelf
for a nicer moment
than the one we have now

and maybe in a month we'll drink it
maybe in a year

all I can think about
is how you say you love me
and yet here I lay
with nothing but fear
that I am that wine bottle
– *the wine bottle is me*

and maybe in a month you'll want me
maybe in a year

but for now
I stay here
on the shelf
waiting for a nicer moment
than the one we have now

waiting for the moment
you finally pour me out
and drink me dry

give me one more moment
to take this all in

– I can't let you go,

I can't watch this end

'goodbye' begins with you

you hit the brakes
and I hit the gas
we must 've been a little too good,
a little too fast

— I do still wish this was something that could last

goodbye.

why do we say goodbye
when not a single part of you leaving
ever felt good?

heartbreak

it's one of those hurts
that sits silently
at the base of my throat
it's there
I can feel it
but it's dormant
until someone asks the ever so daunting question,
"how are you doing?"
and then it comes back to life
– my tears break the silence
and the answer "fine"
sounds like the biggest lie

the unspoken bond

you never said it
but neither could I
so who's to blame
for the look in our eyes?

I know that my love
was something you feared,
and these words alone
won't make you stay
but time is telling me
that it was all just a game

– were you always keeping score?

you held my heart tenderly in your hands
and you let it make a home inside of your own
you held it as gently as you would a flower
or a rose

but then I watched
as you picked
one petal at a time
and suddenly the flower
was left bone dry

– now the only things left
are the thorns
and a blank stare,
and the only words I have left are,
"did you ever actually care?"

he always said I aged like fine wine

— but then I must wonder
if that's his best excuse
for keeping me bottled up
in the back of the cabinet
for when he's ready
to truly enjoy me

forever only sounded sweet
when your name was next to it

– now it tastes as bitter as the lack of love you left me with

one by one
you pulled at my heartstrings
and soon enough
pieces of me unraveled on the floor in front of you

— you stepped over them
like a mess you were trying to avoid
but you can't even see
that you were the one who made it

things I can write about: *you*

I've been writing all sorts of nonsense
since the day that you left
I've been writing about fireplaces that sing
and the way that I watch the trees
I've been jumping in oceans
at 1 in the morning
so that I have something to write about
other than the way that you hurt me

I've kissed strangers in dark alleys
and on rooftops that look over the city
– I've kissed many of them
but it's not always pretty

I've cried
and I've laughed
but none of it
ever seems
to bring you back

*– and my friends keep telling me to be careful
or this world will swallow me whole,*

but can't they see that you did that all on your own?

you break my heart
and I laugh
– *coward,*
at least I have a heart to break

you stay heartless
and still lose the game

the lack of love that you left me with
burned through my body like a wildfire,
just waiting to devastate

    ...did your mother never warn you about playing with fire?

you were always full of danger and disaster
and I had a knack for picking up pieces
of a mess I never made

– how is it that a girl like me ends up playing the love game?

the night you left
silent screams echoed in the darkness,
the street light standing above us went out
and your heart went with it
I think I died a little in that moment
– my whole body went numb
and each bone ached with heartbreak,
sadness seeped through the cracks
and all I could say was,
"are you ever coming back?"

– I know you had such a fetish
for breaking me open,

but aren't you tired of always being heartbroken?

actions speak louder than words

I asked my best friend
how to move on from you
and so she reminded me
that actions speak louder than words
– your actions speak volumes
but your silence screams louder

can you hear it too?

did you ever really love me?

when you left
I had to wrap my entire body
around the idea
that love can be love
and I can be me
without you
and who I thought you could be

– did you ever really love me?

lie to me and tell me you love me

I'd like to ask you why it was so easy for you to leave
after breaking my heart
– *did you not also fall apart?*
I'd like to ask you why you threw us away
– *one last kiss*
and I had no say
I'd like to ask about the ways you missed me
or if there even were any
– I've got a million questions
wrapped up in my heart
and I sincerely believe
that I'll never get
to pull them apart
because every question about you
starts with why
and every part of me wishes
you could tell me one last lie

– *lie to me and tell me you love me,*
for one last night

every time I think about our last night together
my feelings drip onto paper
like the blood that ran down my back

– I know that hurt people, hurt people
but you didn't have to hurt me like that

you said goodbye
faster than my knees
could hit the cold hardwood floor
of that old walk up apartment
that you rented for the summer

– and I didn't know that words
could shatter like glass
but now I must wonder
if that was your voice
or the sound of my knees
breaking the floorboards

and you never apologized
for what you did
but I guess we'll call it even
cause you know I'll always forgive

cammie dennis

I always saw the real you
not who you wanted to be
I always saw through
the things you tried to hide from me

*– and I know it scared you
that I could see more than you wanted me to,*

*but do you think it was easy
to pretend like I didn't know the real you?*

the worst part is
you know how you hurt me
but you still walked away
without a worry
– *I stopped holding my breath*
for any sort of "I'm sorry"

if you want the truth
then let me tell you how you hurt me
you stung like a thousand bees
kissing me on the mouth
you pierced through
the deepest parts of my heart
and showed me no mercy
you took me by my delicate hands
and threw me into
a daze of confusion,
you let me believe
I meant more to you than this

– but if you want the truth
then let me tell you,
the worst part of it all
was to go on living
without you,
at all
and your kind eyes
and your crooked nose
and the dimple that you hate to show
– and I know you gave me no choice
but to love you,

but the truth is,
I don't think I still love you

a moment too long

I wish I could write beautiful words
about the mess that occurs
when people take everything back
and walk out of the life
that they once called their own

I was never the first person to go
or the one to say,
"this isn't working out anymore"
I was always holding on
for a moment too long
hoping that this time
things wouldn't go wrong

I was never the first one
to say "it's time"
or the one to say,
"this isn't right"
I was always holding on
for a moment too long

– and I might not know why people leave
or why I always stay
but one thing I have learned
is to let them walk away

you never called
not once
your silence spoke louder
than any word
you could 've ever said to me

my tears broke the silence
and 'I miss you' rolled off my tongue
in a short text
that went against my better judgment
I wrote,
'I fucking miss you"

the hours between the time I sent it
and when you saw it
felt like a thousand years
and a thousand lies
filled the space in time

my heart began to take over
and my whole body broke in two
but the only thing to fill the space
was the thought of you

– and the heartbreak is nothing new
but I never thought
it would come from you

I thought it was us against the world
but somewhere along the way
it became you against me

        – do you not see what I see?

I would've filled up the empty spaces of you
with every last piece of me
if it meant that you'd stay here with me
– I would've stayed with you forever
if you had asked me to

> *– I think I may always wonder,*
> *why did you never ask me?*

we were a beautiful mess
to say the least,

he was destructive
and I was paper thin

– there was no way I was coming back from this

I don't blame you for not knowing how to love me

— not when the people who you trusted most
were incapable of showing you what love really means

I'm learning to rewrite love
without mentioning your name
so far,
the page is blank

– you are the only thing about love I have ever known

halfway between you and me
were drunken promises
and blank stares,
secrets we vowed to keep
and the bed sheets that we shared
halfway between you and me
there was something left underneath
and I'll always know
there is more to you
than what you tried to show me

but between you and me
our bodies were never enough
to make it through
and now the hole between my ribs
is wide open
for everyone to see
that all of your love
lives inside of me

– I'm sorry I'm not the girl you wanted me to be

"but what if I never stop loving him?
– what if I spend the rest of my life only ever knowing
how to love him?"
she cried.

"well then how lucky are you to love someone for a lifetime,"
the old woman whispered back to her.

january 10, 1:07 pm

I thought of you today
I drove past the flower shop we found
in late October
my hair was shorter then
and my freckles still lingered from the summer
I stopped for a moment
because something was missing
– all of the flowers were gone
and the only thing left
was a sign that read
'no flowers till spring"
I stared at the emptiness
and felt sadness drift through
– there was nothing left for me
at the flower shop
that we once knew
and maybe as time goes on
the flowers will grow back
tall and strong
but the winter months
don't seem to nurture delicate things
– like sunflowers
or you and me

I do wish that I could hear about the memories
from your point of view

– do you ever miss them the way that I do?

the girl you once knew

I'm learning to find comfort in knowing
that you do not know this version of me

not the perfume I wear
or the food I eat
the people I know
and the places I've seen

you don't know about the new scar
on the small of my back
or the book I bought
and then took back
you don't know about the way
that I curl my hair
or put on pink blush
and you definitely don't know about
how I fell in love with someone
who doesn't flinch when we touch

I find comfort in knowing
that you have not met
this version of me
with thicker skin
and stronger teeth
the one who learned
that she can love hard
and love with boundaries
– she kisses strangers for fun
and is full of more love
than the girl you once knew
ever was

(continued)

and as odd as it seems
I find comfort in missing you
and solitude
in not knowing if you miss me

and I know that this is how it goes
when two lost souls
look for love
in impossible places
but there isn't a version of me
that could blame you
for being someone
who never changes

my idea of love
has been so tainted
that my brain convinced me
the words, *'I love you'*
were like giving you the power to kill me,
that to say
'I love you'
was to give you a loaded gun
and an open aim at my heart
and say,
'shoot me
*– my heart is an open target
made just for you."*

but I didn't say it
and you didn't kill me
you just left me with a loaded gun
and nothing left to lose

*– there is nothing left to lose,
when I already lost you*

I'm sitting in the grocery store parking lot
reading poetry about love and lust
and how I feel lost
I think of you
and who you were when you were with me
I loved you then
and I still love you now
but my world seems so turned around
without you in it
my eyes drip tears onto pages of heartbreak
and I wonder if you ever think of me,
– *I bet you still think about me*

I won't apologize for the way that I loved you,
*but I am sorry that you couldn't love me
in the way that I needed you to*

you're the only part of me
that's missing

the age-old question asks:
'is it better to have loved and lost
or to never have loved at all?"

I'd lose you a million times over
if it meant that I could love you just once more
– *do you have to go?*

dear lover,
please stay

– why do people always leave?

yesterday
I told you I miss you
I typed
and retyped
'miss you"
'I miss you"
'I'm missing you"
'I'm missing every part of you"
   – a part of me is missing without you

it's been two months since I've seen your face
47 days to be exact
we spoke few words to each other
we hugged like nice people do to those they love
we dissolved our words in glasses full of whiskey
and you made your rounds
I noticed how convenient it was when you skipped me
but maybe I should be grateful
for the few words we spoke
when you finally noticed
I can't remember what you said
I only remember your laughter
and how consuming it can be

do you remember what we'd say
if I didn't stop seeing your face,
is this all that we will be
– hugs hello and no goodbye?

...I can't remember when we stopped seeing eye to eye

I can't breathe without your touch

plant the flowers
and bury me deep
– *I must be dying without you next to me*

I fucking miss you today
god, no
what a lie
I miss you everyday

– I'm always missing you
and it never seems to stop

I reek of our last conversation
and last night's take out meal
I'm dressed up in stained sweats
and all of the days I've spent
'trying my best'
I'm still full of love
but it's not always lovely
– *even at my worst,*
do you think someone could love me?

thoughts about you

I can't think of a single reason why I love you

− I can't think of a single reason why I don't

every part of my body
screams out for you to love me
but somewhere deep inside
there is a little girl who cries,

"I think I may be unlovable"
"do you ever think you could love me?"

– even when I love hard,
no one ever seems to love me

it's hard for me to love you
and not be able to talk to you

it's even harder to see you happy without me,
even when that's all I want you to be

– happy

I once read that the average time it takes to break a habit is anywhere from 30 to 60 days

– it's been 8 months
and you're still the only thing I can think about

cammie dennis

nothing haunts me more
than the memory
of what it was like
to once be yours

– now all that I have left
are a few photos,
the sand in my shoes
and one half of a heart tattoo

– did I mean nothing to you?

nothing but silence

the memories of us
have become nothing but silence
like a silent disco
but my headphones are broken
and no one is dancing
and everything inside of me is screaming
for you to come back
to come back and hold me
to tell me you love me
but the words you speak to me
have become nothing but silence
and you're nowhere to be found
so I slip away into a crowd
of unwanted strangers
that speak to me
with nothing but silence

I would've lit myself on fire for you
if you had asked me to
but maybe that was my problem all along,

I was on fire for you
and you were the one
holding the match
– you stayed untouched
while my heart turned to black

you had me,
I let you into my weird little world

but then you lost me
– how did you let me go so easily?

some days I wish you had sent me a warning
before you left that Sunday morning
maybe a note on the mirror
or a voicemail on my phone
telling me that you were never coming home
but you packed up your bags
and you left so quick
as if I was just another hit or miss
you didn't leave a trace of you
or a single thing for me
– *now there's nothing left of you,*
except for me

maybe we were just a love story
that was never meant to have a happy ending
maybe we were too good to be true
and now there's nothing left for us to do
– but maybe somewhere along the way
you'll find a piece of me
in an unexpected place
and it'll remind you
of our summer nights,
it'll remind you of all the times
when it was only you and me
and there was nothing between us
but what the night could bring
– *and maybe we were better*
than we ever thought we could be,
but maybe there is more for you
than nights with me

2:00 pm thoughts

it's still you
– *it's always been you*

my problem is that I see every beautiful thing
even on the darkest days
– it's no wonder I held onto you for so long

I saw the light inside of you
that no one wanted to see
and now here I am
looking for what's left of me

cammie dennis

we finally spoke after three months of silence
– he called on a Tuesday,
it was all small talk
but it was better than nothing

I finally saw him after another few months
– we spoke once,
the conversation lasted less than a minute
and I didn't laugh once

– it seems that this is all we will ever be,
strangers that speak in voices that no longer make sense to me

it was August 8th when I told him I loved him,
it was August 30th when he said he doesn't

...can you give me my heart back now?

last night
I dreamt of you
and the night before that
I dreamt of your laugh
and every night before that
I dreamt that you still love me
but every morning
I wake up without your touch
and I can't seem to figure out which is worse:
not having you
or dreaming of what we could be
and then waking up
to an eternal misery

– and now all that we have
are stories full of history

if this is the end
then let it be known
that my body would rather rest
than spend another day alone

– my heart would rather stop
and my mind could be at peace,
*because any day without you
is a day without me*

to hear your laugh in a crowded room
is like hearing my favorite song
play on the radio in a grocery store
– it hits a part of my heart
that I forgot existed,
it hugs my soul
to remind me of your existence

break my heart one more time...

– at least then,
I can still call you mine

here's the thing about us
he likes his coffee black
hot
with no sugar
and a dash of cinnamon
I like matcha
ice cold
with extra honey
and no milk
he likes red wine
and I only drink white
he knows how to love me
but so do I
he says that I sing louder than anyone he has ever heard
yet he dances along each time I scream another word
and I know that if we gave it a chance
he could love me right
but we're two wrongs
and I don't know if that is enough for more than a night
— *just between us*
I was always willing to put up the fight

when did my heart get so heavy?

I can't hate you
or run from you
I can't fight how much I love you

– but that's one thing I do hate,
and loving you seems to be my damned fate

who is your yellow?

sometimes you hear things like
– who is your yellow,
or who is your blue?

all the different colors
represent people
who have come into your life
and changed things for you

– *but to me,*
he was every color

he was my red
and my blue
my green
and my purple
my orange
and my yellow
– he was every color that ever existed,
because he made me feel like I existed

– how do you cope with losing the entire rainbow?

it was a privilege to kiss you in crowded bars
and under the light of midnight stars

it was a privilege to just be near you
but now here I am,
experiencing the privilege
of a life without you

— a life that never would've
crossed my mind
if you hadn't said those last two words,

good bye.

well, fuck

I think I still love you

yes, I must still love you
or my body is lying to me

I do still love you
but that is nothing new
– loving you is my only truth

he loves me, he loves me not enough

it was real for me

– was it ever real for you?

my heart belongs to me

but I think that a part of it
may always live
somewhere within him

your memory dances across my lips
as if it belongs there,
as if it were tattooed on me
without a care

– your memory whispers loudly
as I try to dance with another,

but I know that all he can taste
is the lips of another

for tonight,

I will wipe my tears dry
with the t-shirt you let me borrow
when it was still summer

– this is what getting through it looks like

does summer exist without you?

it's weird the way summer rolls back around
as if you and I never happened
June is still June
and you are still you
but I feel like less of me
without us in July
— do you ever think about what we could be
if we made it past August?

carry my love with you,
wherever you may go

      – my heart will always be a place that you can call home

and I loved you,
despite knowing the worst things about you,
despite all of the things you put me through

– my love for you was as selfless as they come

missing you hurts
but letting you go
– *that's what killed me*

a part of me died,
and you went with it

if I were a bird
I'd fly to you
and tell you how much I love you
but I'm not a bird
no,
I'm just a human being
with a whole life to live
and a lot of love to give
and that must be better than being a bird
– that must be enough,
for what it's worth

and maybe it wasn't your love I needed,
after all

         – maybe it was mine

coming back to me,
with or without you

bittersweet

the only word to describe
the feeling of letting you go

– the only word to describe any feeling about you,
is bittersweet

maybe in the next lifetime
it'll be you
– but for this one,
I have to choose me

now I see that you had to hurt me
for me to see all of the things
that I never wanted you to be

– even if it kills me
I have to let you go
because my life is meant to be
so much more

I would've dragged my own name
through the mud
to keep yours clean

the problem with that
is that it goes against
all of the love
that I have for me
– and the problem with you
is that you would've let me

if the highest form of love is consideration
then did you ever really love me?

— I know how I considered you
but I know better
than to think
you ever considered me

it takes more than love to make it last
and I wish that weren't the truth
but here I am,
leaving our love in the past

– my love is the only part of us
that was ever meant to last

I was made to love

...but not like this

do you think forgiveness is a part of loving someone?

I forgive you
but now I must forget you

– if I don't
you'll keep hurting me
and I'll keep letting you

he loves me, he loves me not enough

I drove past a field of sunflowers today
– I didn't think of you once

I'd like to think that's progress

162

the seasons change and so do we

fall
where you ended
and I began

winter
was it the cold of the night
or your cold heart
that made you walk away?

spring
the flowers grew and so did I

summer
like any other year
it came and it went
and the only thing left
were the memories we keep
and the tan lines on my back

– now I understand why seasons never last

for the first time in my life,
I give up
– I give up on you
and I give up on us

I can't keep fighting
for people to stay
and losing myself
every time someone walks away

– I can't keep losing myself,

so I have to lose you

I always saw the best in him
all of the parts that no one else could see
I always saw the beautiful things
that I wanted him to be
– *I always saw him*
and he saw me,
but the truth is
he doesn't know what love means
and the only thing he does know
is how to hurt me
– but the truth is
that the truth hurts,

and even he knows
my love was never something he deserved

love was never a four letter word to me

it was fire pits crackling on the beach
and smoking joints on a porch
it was never ending laughter
and a wine bottle without a cork

he always knew just how to love me
and with that
he knew how to break me

he always thought his love might fix me
but he wasn't a joint
or a wine bottle

he was a boy that smiled on occasion
and kissed my forehead with apprehension
and I guess he knew how to build a fire
he just didn't know how to keep the flames alive

sometimes you have to say
– *there is nothing else I could've done*
to change the outcome of us
even through tear soaked sentences
and wilted blue eyes
you have to be brave enough to know
that the bravest thing you ever did
was let them go

you were the hardest lesson I had to learn
– but now that's all you can be,
a lesson learned

it's true when they say that love is blind
– *and letting you go was the only thing I needed*
to see that you were never really mine

to love someone
and let them go
– that is a strength
unlike anything
you could ever know

– that is strength
and courage
and loving yourself
despite all of it,

that is love
in its most sacred form

you are not a villain in my story
you are just a boy with broken plans
and shaky hands
and a heart that wanted this to last
you remind me of winter days when the sun still shines
and the cold can only be felt on the inside
you are not an unforgivable person
or someone that deserves to hurt
you are just a boy who needed someone to hold your heart
and if I ever see you again
I will hold you with the grace of my hands
to remind you that I am here
and I cannot be bothered to go anywhere
because you are not a villain
or a mistake that I made
you are a boy that once gave me everything
you made flowers grow inside my lungs
and gave me the voice to sing my song
you are someone who deserves to love
and be loved in return
and I mean that in every sense of the word
– you are the sun to me
even when I cannot see you
I always feel you
and if I ever see you again
I will never be able to leave you

it is lucky
to know what it feels like
to experience love
outside of this body of mine,
it is anything but ordinary

> *– and now I must thank you*
> *for allowing me*
> *to feel something extraordinary*

loving you was never a waste

to love you for a time
was only a pleasure

– and the pleasure was all mine

I wish we could've been two people
who beat the odds,
two people
who made it through it all
– but sometimes beautiful things must end
and the odds will never be in our favor,
sometimes people can only love you
with half of their heart
and you don't always realize it
until you get back to the start,
the start of you

– because you are someone
who deserves to be loved
wholeheartedly,
you are someone
who deserves love
in it's entirety

I still hope my love changed you

– in one way or another

I do hope you remember me with fondness
and not like the rest of them do
I hope that when you see my face
across a crowded bar
you're reminded of the girl that you once knew
I hope that something in you feels free
when you see me
and maybe our eyes won't whisper
that we are still meant to be
but they will always tell the secrets
that we could never keep
I hope the left side of your bed is always full
and the back side of your pillow is always cold
and I hope that somewhere along the way
your heart finds a place that it can call home
I hope that every birthday of yours
is filled with everything you could ever dream of
and I hope your days are spent with someone
that knows how to show you love

– and I do hope that one of these days
you think of me,

and you're reminded of the nights
when we fit perfectly

and on that last day
his heart closed
and so did the door to us

– and despite all of the hurt
I am still here
with a wide open heart
and two ears that listen
to the people around me
who remind that what comes next
is better than anything
my heart could have dreamed

what comes next,
– it was made for me

note to self:

it's not that he didn't love you
in fact,
everyone could see how he adored you,
but that was the problem
– he never knew how to love himself
so the idea of loving you
scared him more than anything else

the letter I never sent, the words I never said

you were my first love
the only one who ever saw me
for who I truly was
you turned my heart into something softer
than I had ever seen before
– you made the darkest parts of me
brighter than before
you were my first love
and I wish this could last
but you showed me
that when you love hard
there's no going back
you were my first love
the only one to ever see me cry
you held me in your heart
and led me through the night
you were my first love
and I love you so
but the truth is
first loves don't always grow
– they don't always last longer than a summer
or make it through December
and so if this is where we part ways
know that not a day goes by
when I don't think of your face,
– and I know this must be where we part ways
but please know that if ever you need me
I'll always be one call away

this is me letting go
this is me letting go of you
– this is me
and you
letting go of each other

> *– because it was lovely*
> *that out of all of the people*
> *in this world*
> *we ended up together*
> *for a night*
> *or two,*
> *we ended up*
> *under the light of the moon*
> *as one,*
> *and we watched the rise*
> *of the morning sun*
> *– we had our days*
> *and we had our fights*
> *and we had our love*
> *to hold us through the night*

but now it's time
that I let you go
– now it's time
that I let my love grow

someone can love you
with everything that they have,
but that doesn't mean it has to be enough for you

you are allowed to find the love
that loves you right
– you are allowed to give up the fight

mundane activities

it is the first Saturday of April
and the world is lit up by several rays of sunshine
there is a slight breeze
and the clouds are moving at an unknown speed
I haven't stopped crying since December
but today feels unlike the others
the rays of sunshine whisper their whereabouts
across my pale skin
and my heart opens
like a flower that has begun to bloom
I sit and contemplate the last four months of my life
– *I have my books*
and a couple of smokes
I have the rays of sunshine
and a pile of words to sort through
my mind is always moving
but for today
I must stop to think,
I must recognize where I am
and who I have become
– *for today*
I will move like the sun
and show myself love

and now I will fall into the space
of only needing myself

– the sun will still shine without you

love

I would like you to paint the word 'love'
across my forehead
and then call me by it

– you will remember me not just by name
but by what I am

I love
without regard for
ever being loved in return

        – and what a beautiful thing that is

don't ever be embarrassed
for the way that you fought
for what you loved
– *learn from it,*
but don't ever let it make you feel
like you were less
because of it

I find the truest act of self love
is to choose yourself
when faced with the decision
of loving yourself
or another

– the love that you have for yourself is eternal

the one where she saves herself

I was always waiting
for my knight in shining armor
to come here and hold me,
to show up and save me
– someone to tell me
that I might just make it out alive
with someone else by my side

but there was no knight in shining armor
to come in and save me
no,
there was only me
and that must be enough
to just be

– it must be enough
to only have me

you are so much more
than the sum of your past loves
you are more than the feeling
of never being enough,
you are more than anyone
could ever believe
– *now go out and find*
who you could be

find out who you are
and what you love
find out that you are far more
than what once was
find what sets your soul on fire
and then live in it
– find what makes you feel beautiful
and then be it

I am a sensitive being
living in an insensitive world

*– it is no wonder that my heart has been broken
so many times*

I want to talk to strangers
and kiss people that I love with no remorse
I want to fall in love
and be loved back
and I want to be someone that people do things for,
not the one who's always doing things for other people
I want to roam the streets
without holding my keys tightly in my fist
and dance in a crowd
without worrying about the men that are around
I want to drift off into the middle of the ocean
with no goodbye
and I want to feel free and alive,
but I am so terribly held back
by the world around me
and I so effortlessly hate it
for what it's done to me

and I do wonder if there will be a day
that I can do all of the things that I say
but then I must wonder
– will I always be waiting for that day?

when I love
it's nothing like slow drip coffee
or Sunday mornings
it's four shots of espresso
and dancing on countertops
when I love
I spill my guts on the pages of notebooks
and draw pretty pictures all over the walls of my home
when I love
I love with every piece of my being
– *my love is not made for the faint of heart*
so please do not expect any less of me

I have always been kind and beautiful

yes,
I have

I am still kind
and beautiful
and many other things
– even without you here,
I am still me

yes,
I am
– and what a wonderful thing to be

there is no love
without you,
my dear

– there is no art
without you,
my love

I have so much love living inside of me

and I know there will come a day
when someone comes around
to find it,
but until then
– *in my heart*
is where I will hide it

to the one who loves me next:

there may come a day
when you have to meet the boy who broke my heart
the one who inspired
all of the art
if there is one thing I ask you to do
treat him with kindness
he knows what he's got to lose
don't give him an eye roll
or a punch in the arm
he already has
one too many scars
if he asks you about me
tell him that I am happy
and in love
but don't let him know too much
he is a kind soul
with a broken compass
and if he sees me with you
I know how he'll judge it
he is more than what meets the eye
and he is anything but shy
so when he hugs me hello
please don't forget
that we already said our goodbye
there is nothing left to say
between that boy and me,
and I know how he hurts
but he can't be my responsibility

– I might've loved him with every part of me
but the girl I was back then
is no longer a part of me

someday soon
I know I'll see you
I'll still be wearing the same smile
I wore when I was with you
my hair will still be just as red
and maybe twice as long
my freckles might be faded
but my heart will remain the same
someday soon
I know I'll see you
and I'll be happy to tell you
that I am happy without you
someday soon
I know I'll see you
and I'll be hesitant to tell you
that I have fallen in love with someone new
someone that is so unlike you
someday soon
I will fall out of love with you
and I know that when I see you
I'll have the courage to tell you
that it was never going to be you
– *not for me,*
even though I wanted it to be
and someday soon
I hope you fall in love with someone new
but someday soon,
I hope you learn how to love yourself too

coming home

my heart is my home
but I will leave it open
for the world to see

I will scream 'love'
at the top of my lungs
until the day that I die

– *I will let love back in,*
but only when it's time

the kindest thing a boy ever said to me:

people spend a lifetime looking for a girl like you

– thank you for giving me the strength to stand back up,
after all of the times I have been knocked down

love is my religion
and I pray with both hands that I make it out alive

– *it's no wonder I need love to survive*

love her

I feel it all
and I feel it so deeply
I feel everything
with every part of my body

– my body has no remorse
for how much she feels
but still,
I love her
for everything that she is

the muse

I put my pen to paper
and I let the words trickle out
like a waterfall of emotions

I am the muse of my own creation
– I am the poem,
just waiting to be written

healing my own heart

I sing,
loudly
and in every beautiful place that I can find

I dance,
freely
to nurture the space between my heart and my mind

I write
and then I write some more
and somewhere in the mess of it all
I find myself on the bathroom floor

and so I cry
and then I cry some more
I let myself feel it all
and then feel some more

– but somewhere in me,
I am still alive with it all

would you rather hold a rose by its petals or its thorns?

you ask me how I have so much love inside of me
– you say it bursts from the seams
for everyone to see
you ask me,
"even after all of the thunder
and all of the rain
and all of the times that they've tried to make you tame,
how are you not tainted with hatred?"

and so I must ask you the question
I so often ask myself:
– *would you rather hold a rose by its petals or its thorns?*

I am a lover
without a lover

– and that is my superpower

I love with every part of me

and I deserve to be loved by someone
who loves every part of me,
with every part of them

– I deserve to be loved back

pretty like you

and when the little girl in me cries out,
"why can't I be pretty like them?"

I hold her in my arms
and whisper,
"baby, you get to be pretty like you
– and that is something that nobody can take from you."

a letter to myself

you are not your scars
or the burdens of those you love
you are not a broken heart
or days without the sun
you are not tattered hands
or broken promises
and you are not the person you were
when all of this started
you are not the person you were
three years ago
or even yesterday
you are a beautiful creature
with love running through your veins,
you have light pouring out of your soul
and the words that you speak
make people feel whole
– *and you are kind*
and beautiful
and unusually bold,
and souls like you
are what make this world
feel a little less cold

to be a woman
with a soft heart
and a powerful mind

– that is magic in my eyes

mirror image

I smiled at the reflection
and the reflection smiled back at me

– thank you for being you
and letting me
be me

if you do one thing for me

listen to your heart,
– *it will whisper secrets that your mind cannot*

it's all love,
from here on out

– it's all about loving me,
without you

from my heart to yours, with love

about the author

Cammie Dennis was born and raised in Orange County, California. She attended the University of Colorado, Boulder where she received her Bachelor's degree. After college, she decided to pursue her dream of being a writer. She hopes that she can change the hearts of others with her words – the same way that her favorite authors changed her heart with their own.

–

Find her on social media:

@cammiedennis

Printed in Great Britain
by Amazon

32659006R00126